FEARLESS

PAHLINE HARDING

0

CONTENTS

Perfect love casts out fear   8
Whom shall I fear?   9
Do not fear or be intimidated by the New Year   10
Do not fear the mistakes of last year   11
Do not fear going into a New Year alone   12
Do not fear lack of resources in the coming year   13
Do not fear the changes ahead   14
Do not fear being single another year   15
Do not fear difficulties in life   16
Do not fear the fire of testing   17
Do not fear being rejected by God   18
Do not fear being on your own   19
Do not fear the vast army that has surrounded you   20
Do not fear barrenness   21
Do not fear man   22
Do not fear physical attack   23
Do not fear the death of a loved one   24
Do not fear death   25
Do not fear attending a funeral or court case   26
Do not fear separation from a loved one   28
Do not fear financial downturn   29
Do not fear lack   30
Do not fear the future   31
Do not fear change   32
Do not fear financial lack   33

Do not fear others excelling 34

Do not fear speaking for God 35

Do not fear speaking in court 36

Do not fear city riots 37

Do not fear people walking out of your life. 38

Do not fear the supernatural 39

Do not fear losing your mind 40

Do not fear death 41

Do not fear sickness 42

Do not fear missing your opportunity for success 43

Do not fear those who curse you 45

Do not fear not having enough to eat or drink 46

Do not fear the command to go! 47

Do not fear lack 48

Do not fear sudden disaster 49

Do not fear perplexing or uncertain times 50

Do not fear God letting you down 51

Do not fear sleepless nights 52

Do not fear stepping out and doing something new 53

Do not fear floods, landslides or earthquakes 54

Do not fear your own weakness 55

Do not fear using your talents 56

Do not fear war 57

Do not fear being left behind 58

Do not fear God's guidance 59

Do not fear being put to shame   60
Do not fear what is coming on the world   61
Do not fear losing your parents   62
Do not fear physical pain   63
Do not fear the memory of pain   64
Do not fear flooding   65
Do not fear failing God   66
Do not fear losing faith in God   67
Do not fear losing friends   68
Do not fear the power of sin   69
Do not fear torture or persecution   70
Do not fear the dark   72
Do not fear your enemies   73
Do not fear carrying out God's plans   74
Do not fear inadequacy   75
Do not fear being exiled or rejected   76
Do not fear what you are going to say   77
Do not fear spiritual darkness   78
Do not fear getting out of the boat   79
Do not fear loneliness   80
Do not fear the trauma of your past   81
Do not fear getting hurt again   82
Do not fear liars   83
Do not fear those in authority over you   84
Do not fear losing your children   85

Do not fear sharing the gospel	86
Do not fear global warming	87
Do not fear heart attacks	88
Do not fear the call of Leadership	89
Do not fear moving to a new area	90
Do not fear illness or disease	91
Do not fear not being accepted by God	92
Do not fear being cast away from God	93
Do not fear other people's success or promotion	94
Do not fear creatures big or small	95
Do not fear curses	96
Do not fear God's promises to you will die	98
Do not fear putting your dream on the altar	99
Do not fear temptation becoming too strong for you	100
Do not fear someone stealing your dream	101
Do not fear failure	102
Do not fear going back	103
Do not fear acting on what you believe	104
Do not fear false accusations	105
Do not fear speaking for God because of age	106
Do not fear the fiery trial	107
Do not fear lack of strength	108
Do not fear going back to work	109
Do not fear Jesus' return	110
Do not fear cancer	111

Do not fear discouragement 113

Do not fear depression 114

Do not fear transition 115

Do not fear Gethsemane 116

Do not fear hunger 117

Do not fear your sons or daughters moving away 118

Do not fear those who plan evil against you 119

Do not fear delays to prayer 120

Do not fear stepping out in later years 121

Do not fear being hemmed in 122

FEARLESS

'I will tell you whom to fear,
fear God and God alone'

PERFECT LOVE CASTS OUT FEAR. 1 JOHN 4:18

Those who know their God shall be strong and do exploits!

The reason you fear is that you do not believe God loves you enough to keep you, protect you or provide for you in every situation. If you truly understood the Love God has for you and how much He is committed to you, you would not entertain fear.

God will turn even your worst situations around for good if you love, trust and obey Him, God's plan for you is to walk in absolute peace and love, free from fear of any kind and filled with the power of the Holy Spirit.

Commit to being fearless from this day forward.

WHOM SHALL I FEAR?

I sought the Lord and He heard me and delivered me from ALL my fears. Psalm 34:9

Is it possible to walk free of all fears in this day of trouble, trauma and global unrest? Absolutely! There is no reason to fear anything or any man.

God says in Psalm 46:10 'Be still and know that I AM God.' There is no fear found in the presence of God, only faith!

Do not fear or be intimidated by the the New Year

Moses said, "Be strong and courageous, for the Lord Himself goes before you and will be with you."
Deuteronomy 31:7-8

Commit the New Year into God's hands and rest assured that Jesus will go before you. He will be there ahead of you. Commit every appointment and commitment of the New Year to God. He is faithful to keep and bless all you put into His hands.

Do not fear the mistakes of last year

He is able to save completely those who come to God through Him, because He always lives to intercede for them. Hebrews 7:25

Jesus is able to save you from the mistakes and failings of the past year. It is time to trust God for a New Year. He will work all things together for your good. Believe God's word that if you confess your sins He is faithful and just and will forgive you and cleanse you from any unrighteousness.

Move on in the knowledge that God's plan for your life is still very much in operation. He will redeem last year for you as you walk in obedience this year. He will restore any part of the year that the locust has eaten.

Do not fear going into a New Year

ALONE

God sets the lonely in families. Psalm 68:6

Commit this year into the hands of a loving God who is in control of every detail of your life. He has kept you until this day and will continue to keep you tomorrow.

He is your provider and will provide the right person or persons at the right time. There is an appointed time for you to see your desires and prayers met. Begin to imagine the kind of people you want in your life and expect God to open the right doors of opportunity to meet new people this year.

Lonely but never alone!

Do not fear lack of resources in the coming year

You open Your hand and satisfy the desires of every creature.
Psalm 145:16

The Lord is my Shepherd I shall not be in want. Psalm 23:1

Do not fear lack this year. Jesus came to give you life and give it in abundance. He has promised to supply all your needs according to His riches in glory. Do not be afraid of tomorrow, God is already there and has prepared provision for you.

Never, never, never from this day worry about provision!

DO NOT FEAR THE CHANGES AHEAD

Do not be terrified; do not be discouraged, for the Lord your God will be with you wherever you go. Joshua 1:9

God will be in the coming changes for your work, house, family or location. Banish fear because God has promised you wisdom and guidance for the coming year.

God is your guide and will guide you even unto death. Do not fear what tomorrow may bring for God is in your tomorrow!

DO NOT FEAR BEING SINGLE ANOTHER YEAR.

It is not good for the man to be alone. Genesis 2:18

Give the burden of wanting to meet someone to God for He did not design man or woman to be alone and His desire for you is to have companionship. If you are single give God the details of the person you would like to meet. Make it clear and write it down. Start seeing yourself with someone.

If you are separated find out ways of making new friends in a secure environment, and keep up with old friends. Fill your life with purpose and do not entertain fearful thoughts of being alone.

God will make a way for you where there seems to be no way

DO NOT FEAR DIFFICULTIES IN LIFE

Fear not, for I have redeemed you; When you pass through the waters I will be with you. Isaiah 43:1-3

Do not worry or be overwhelmed at the difficulties you are facing. Focus on the solution and not on the problem. Look to the one who is able to bring you out of your troubles and lift you out of the sea of difficulties.

'When the waves mount up, You still them.'
Psalm 89:9

Jesus said to the waves, 'Quiet! Be still!' and it was completely calm. Mark 4:39

DO NOT FEAR THE FIRE OF TESTING

Fear not, when you walk through the fire you will not be burned. Isaiah 43: 2

The fiery trials are sent to refine you, not destroy you. When you come through this test you will be as gold refined in the fire. Those things you wanted to be free of will melt away in the fire.

But God will not allow you to be tested or tempted more than you can bear. At the right time He will lift you up and promote you.

Do not fear being rejected by God

'I have chosen you and not rejected you, so do not fear for I Am with you' Isaiah 41:9
Whoever comes to me I will never drive away.
John 6:37

Jesus promised He would never drive away those who came to Him. God calls you to Himself in your distress, hunger or hurt. Do not stay out of His presence because of how you feel. He wants to share intimately in your life for He cares for you. When you go to God He has promised to receive you and will never, never reject you.

Draw near to God today and He will draw near to you!

Do not fear being on your own

Jesus said, "Dear woman here is your son," and to the disciple, "Here is your mother." John 19: 26

God made you for relationship. He made you to be in community with other people.

A life lived for others is a fulfilled life. Think of ways you can be a blessing to someone today. Maybe a family member, a friend or someone at your church. As you sow into others' lives around you, God will open the right connections for you.

Bless someone today and sow into your future!

DO NOT FEAR THE VAST ARMY THAT HAS SURROUNDED YOU

Do not be afraid or discouraged because of this vast army.
For the battle is not yours but God's.
Take up your positions; stand firm and see the deliverance the Lord will give you. 2 Chronicles 20:15-17

Are you surrounded by problems on every side and feel hemmed in with no way out?
There is a way out of your situation, it is called 'thanksgiving and praise'.

Your praise goes before deliverance and prepares the way for God's salvation. Greater is He that is in you than He that is in the world.

DO NOT FEAR BARRENNESS

---◆---

So in the 'course of time' Hannah conceived and gave birth to a son. 1 Samuel 1:20

Many women in the Bible cried out for a child and God heard and answered the desires of their heart. In the course of time, Hannah's prayer was answered. There is always a 'course of time' with God. Do not look at how long your 'course of time' has been, but keep believing.

There may be more than one way to have your desire met. If you cannot have a child of your own you may consider, further treatment, adopting or simply resting on the promises of God.

DO NOT FEAR MAN

Fear of man will prove to be a snare. Proverbs 29:25

Fear of people will ensnare you and block you from moving on in your life. Do not fear what man can do, say, think or threaten. You have not been given a spirit of intimidation but one of love, power and a sound mind. Perfect love casts out fear and the only way to overcome your enemies is to find a way to love them.

Remember, love is not a feeling but an action. The smallest action of love towards someone can release you from fear.

DO NOT FEAR PHYSICAL ATTACK

Do not be afraid of those who kill the body but after that can do no more. Luke 12:4

God tells you not to fear man's ability to hurt you. The antidote against the fear of man, is to fear God.

Do not allow images of physical attack to dominate your thought life. If fear presents itself then either pray, praise or speak in your prayer language until your focus changes.

God can and will deliver you in your hour of need, if you trust and fear God above all else.

DO NOT FEAR THE DEATH OF A LOVED ONE

Where, death is your victory? Where, death is your sting? 1 Corinthians 15:55

Do you fear the death of someone close to you? God says He is near to the brokenhearted and heals their wounds. God has promised to give you comfort and joy instead of sorrow.

The death of a loved one does not have to overwhelm you. God will give you the strength to come through the death of a loved one in victory and peace. Give your fears to God and He will deliver you. Jesus has overcome the sting of death.

Nothing is impossible with God. Underneath you are the everlasting arms and they will carry you through this painful time of grief and loss.

DO NOT FEAR DEATH

For I am convinced that neither death nor life, will be able to separate us from the love of God that is in Christ Jesus our Lord. Romans 8:38

Have you had a near death experience or a trauma that leaves you in fear of death? Bring the fear to God. Repent of the fear of death and command the fear of death to leave you in the powerful name of Jesus Christ. Or ask a minister to pray with you.

If someone has spoken death over you get the scriptures out and speak life over yourself.

Jesus is our life, both in this world and in the next, so do not fear the transition but put your hand in His hand and He will uphold you.

DO NOT FEAR ATTENDING A FUNERAL OR COURT CASE

Are you fearful of attending an occasion of unknown dynamics?

Do not fear what may happen.
1. Commit everything to God. Especially the things that are worrying you about the occasion.
2. Believe that no weapon fashioned against you will prosper or come to pass.
3. Soak the whole occasion in the blood of Jesus.
4. Ask for faith in place of fear.
5. Do not fear man or their words or their rejection of you.
6. Go in the peace and love of God.

'Do not be afraid, I am your shield
and your very great reward.'
Genesis 15:1

DO NOT FEAR SEPARATION FROM A LOVED ONE

Nothing will be able to separate us from the love of God that is in Christ Jesus our Lord.
Romans 8:38

Do you fear separation from a spouse, loved one, a child, a job, church or friends.

God says, do not fear any separation because nothing will separate you from His love. God will either bring the people who leave you back into your life, or He will bring others along to fill their place. Alternatively He will give you more of Himself in place of those you have lost.

He has promised He will never, never leave you.

DO NOT FEAR FINANCIAL DOWNTURN

The Lord be exalted who delights in the well-being of His servant. Psalms 35:27

God has ordained for you to walk in prosperity, not in lack. He has promised to provide for you. Never, never, never from this day worry about provision.

You are going up and not going down. Speak the word of God over your circumstances. Agree with God's word and not with your negative situation.

Prosperity means success in every area of your life; relationally, financially, spiritually, emotionally and physically.

Do not fear lack

My God will meet all your needs according to His glorious riches in Christ Jesus. Philippians 4:6
The Lord is my shepherd I shall not be in want.
Psalm 23:1

The Lord has made provision for you so that you do not have to live in fear of what you need.

The answer is to rest in God and His promises for you and hear what He would say to you.

The Lord gives you the power to get wealth.

When the brook dried up for Elijah, God sent ravens to feed him. The second time his resource dried up a widow provided for him.

God does not always provide for you in the same way. Be sensitive to God's leading for the particular way He wants to provide for you today.

Do not fear the future

Jesus said, "I go and prepare a place for you." John 14:3
See, I am sending an angel ahead of you to bring you to the place I have prepared. Exodus 23:20

Do not fear the future for God is already there!

God has gone ahead of you to provide places, people, homes and work for you. There are good things stored up for you ahead so do not give into the fear of the enemy. Weeping may last a night but in the morning there is joy.

No one has seen or imagined what God has planned for those who love Him.

DO NOT FEAR CHANGE

I the Lord do not change. Malachi 3:6

Do not fear the changing seasons of life. Do not fear going to University, getting married, needing work, having children, children leaving home, losing parents, sickness, moving to a new area, getting older or any other life situation.

God is the God who does not change and He is the same yesterday today and forever. He has promised never to fail you or leave you on your own.

Trust God for the changing seasons of your life. He will literally cause all things to work together for your good.

Do not fear financial lack

Do not be anxious about anything, but in everything, by prayer and petition with thanksgiving present your requests to God. Philippians 4:6

God uses dry and barren times in your life to activate new creative flows within you. There are untapped ideas, resources and potentials within you that need a certain amount of pressure to flow out. Maybe in this season of lack God may encourage you to step out and try something new.

Maybe you have had the dream to start a business, write a book or step into a calling. Barren times define what we really want in life and help us prioritise our goals. Give Him your worries today and ask Him for creative ideas.

DO NOT FEAR OTHERS EXCELLING

Peter asked 'Lord what about him?' Jesus answered, 'What is that to you? You must follow Me'. John 21:22

Do not fear the success of others but find the purpose for which God made you and fulfill it. There is a plan, work and call of God that is uniquely yours and nobody else can fulfill it. Every one has been given specific talents and gifts by God and you are only responsible for your call and talents and not anyone else's.

There is no need to feel threatened by someone else's call or gift. Check out your life and see if there is any disobedience or laziness that is causing you to fall short of the amazing destiny God has for your life!

Do not fear speaking for God

Do not say, " I am only a child. You must go to everyone I send you to and say whatever I command you." Jeremiah 1:7

God will give you the words to say if you have the courage to open your mouth and speak for Him. God says, 'Open your mouth and I will fill it.'

Do not fear looking foolish or feeling self–conscious, but be God conscious.

Keep close to God and His word and He will use your mouth to bless many. Streams of living water will flow from you to refresh others.

Do not fear speaking in court

Do not worry about what you are going to say ahead of time for I will be with you and give you the words to say. Matthew 10:19

If you are facing a court case do not worry what you are going to say. Bring any fears to God and trust Him to be with you and anoint the words you speak. Do not fear your opponent or be intimidated by their words. God defends those who are His.

God promises to shut the mouths of liars. Your responsibility is to tell the truth in court and God will take care of your opponents. Ask God to give you His wisdom and authority.

DO NOT FEAR CITY RIOTS

Mockers stir up a city but wise men turn away anger.
Proverbs 29:8

Do not fear the mob spirit. Keep a wise and peaceful spirit. Commit the situation to God and declare scripture in the face of any intimidation. Take authority over the spirit of anarchy and lawlessness and be open to what the spirit of God is saying to you. Do not be tempted to embrace the spirit of anger that manifests, but come back in a different spirit.

Ask God to put His angels around you and your family and keep them safe.

Greater is the one in you than the one in the world.
1 John 4:4

DO NOT FEAR PEOPLE WALKING

OUT OF YOUR LIFE

Jesus said I will never leave you or forsake you.
Hebrews 13:5
When my mother and father abandon me the Lord will
receive me. Psalm 27:10
Everyone deserted me but the Lord stood by me.
2 Timothy 4: 16

Do not fear people walking out of your life; when one door closes another one opens. God's plan is not to leave you desolate and empty, but to give you an opportunity for growth and new blessings. People walk in and out of our lives all the time. When you feel most deserted you never know who is about to walk into your life.

God may bring the person who walked away back into your life at another time. Meanwhile release them into God's hands. Many times God brings someone else along who can be a greater blessing.

DO NOT FEAR THE SUPERNATURAL

Jesus said 'I have given you authority over all the power of the enemy; nothing shall by any means harm you. Luke 10:18

Do not fear encountering the supernatural; God is supernatural. Do not be afraid of the Holy Spirit, angels, demons or the gifts of the Holy Spirit. God is in control of the supernatural dimension and Jesus has all authority.

The Bible is a good source of wisdom and understanding on the supernatural realm. As you study the word of God you will understand the power in the name of Jesus and any fear will leave. Be filled with the Holy Spirit for He will empower you and give you understanding of who you are in Christ.

DO NOT FEAR LOSING YOUR MIND

For God did not give you a spirit of fear but a spirit of power love and a sound mind. 2 Tim 1:7

Have you got a family history of mental illness, breakdowns or anxieties? Are you stressed or emotionally challenged? Take the word of God as a sword and cut yourself free from the lies and fears of the enemy and any hereditary ties. Quote 2 Timothy 1 verse 7 and do not allow the enemy to intimidate you. The word of God says 'Perfect love casts out all fear.' Allow God's love to saturate you afresh and drive out any fear or worry that overwhelms your mind.

Remind yourself that God is in control of your life and nothing can separate you from His love. Cast all your care on Him for He cares for you. The peace of God will guard your heart and mind.

Do not fear death

What can separate us from the love of God? For I am convinced that neither death nor life will be able to separate us from the love of God Romans 8:38

God is the author of life and death and we are in the palms of His hands. Jesus overcame death for us on the cross.
1. Maybe you had a near death experience.
2. Maybe you witnessed someone dying.
3. Maybe you were threatened with death, verbally or physically.
4. Maybe you have been given a negative doctor's report.

Give your fears of death to God and repent for not trusting God with your life. Command the spirit of fear of death to 'GO!' in the name of Jesus. Then ask God to fill you with the Holy Spirit and faith.

Do not fear sickness

---◆---

By His wounds we are healed Isaiah 53:5

Do not give into fear over negative symptoms in your body or by a doctor's diagnosis. Take the word of God and saturate yourself with verses on healing from the word of God. God's word will counteract any negative diagnoses.

Your condition may not kill you but fear of your condition is dangerous. Job said what he feared had come upon him! God's word tells us to banish the troubles from our bodies.

Command all sickness to leave your body and keep believing God's word over and above the lies of the enemy. You have all authority over the enemy and nothing shall by any means harm you!

DO NOT FEAR MISSING YOUR OPPORTUNITY FOR SUCCESS

God will repay you for the years the locust's have eaten. Joel 2:25

Has life passed you by and you worry you may have missed your opportunity? Remember it is never too late with God. Caleb asked for his inheritance when he was eighty and Abraham came into his promise at a hundred years old. Jacob moved geographically and started again with his family in his latter years.

God has not forgotten you. There is always another chance with God and He will strengthen and refine you for His purposes. Try the doors: one will open for you to fulfill the longing of destiny within you. It is never too late with God! It is only over when He says it is over!

'Do not be afraid to go, for I will make you into a great nation there.'
Genesis 46:3

Do not fear those who curse you

How can a man curse what God has blessed?
Numbers 23:8

Man cannot curse what God has blessed and you are blessed. As long as you walk in obedience to God no curse of the enemy can come to fruition.

Proverbs 26:2 says, 'An undeserved curse does not come to rest.'

Man's words against you cannot hurt you. God will turn them around for a blessing for you. Resist the need to defend yourself; God will defend you. You are anointed and appointed by Almighty God and He will defend and protect you. The mouths of liars shall be shut.

Do not fear not having enough to eat or drink

Do not worry what you will eat or drink.
Matthew 6:25

If you are faithful in your giving to the house of God then expect miracles to happen and expect God to provide for you.

God is faithful and King David said he had never seen the righteous forsaken or their children begging bread. God provided different ways of feeding Elijah. First He sent ravens and then He led a poor widow to feed him. Ask and it shall be given unto you.

Do not be surprised where your provision comes from.

DO NOT FEAR THE COMMAND TO GO!

If God says 'Go' but you do not know where to go do not fear. Wait calmly on the Lord to show you the next step. If you believe there is a move ahead then prepare as much as possible and check it out with those over you.

Tell God you do not want to go without His presence, God has promised to guide you with His eye. So do not be afraid to step out and move on because God will open or close doors as you step out in obedience to Him.

Abraham stepped out not knowing where he was going but God led him into his destiny.

Do not fear lack

My God shall supply all your needs according to His glorious riches in Christ Jesus. Philippians 4:19

Paul said, 'I know what it is to be in need, and I know what it is to have plenty, I have learned the secret of being content in any and every situation, whether well fed or hungry, whether living in plenty or in want.'

Your need may be physical, spiritual or emotional but God has promised that you would lack no good thing as you walk uprightly. Bring your needs to God today and trust that He wants to meet those needs. Be proactive and sow a seed into the area of your need and see the harvest you want come back to you.

DO NOT FEAR SUDDEN DISASTER

The Lord will be your confidence and will keep your foot from being snared.
When you lie down you will not be afraid for your sleep will be sweet. Proverbs 3:25

You need not fear or panic at sudden bad news or disaster. God is in control and has promised He will keep you in that hour and make a way of escape for you.

Learn to listen to the shepherd's voice. Then at a moment's notice you will know when He says, 'Fear not and follow me'. He will lead you out of disaster as you trust in Him.

Do not fear perplexing or uncertain times

So you can say with confidence 'The Lord is my helper I will not be afraid.' Hebrews 13:5

In times of stress or uncertainty when all you can do is cry, 'help Lord', He is there. God has promised He will never leave you or fail you. When you don't know which way to turn next, simply trust His word. God is faithful and will not leave you helpless, He will come to you and give you His peace.

It is important to learn to trust God in times of uncertainty and say like Jehoshaphat, I don't know what to do but I am looking to you for help. It is not wrong to face uncertain times but it is important to keep bringing your situation to God until there is clarity.

DO NOT FEAR GOD LETTING YOU DOWN

If you faint in the day of adversity your faith is small.
Proverbs 24:10

God promised that those who trusted in Him would never be let down or put to shame.

Do not look at your resources and faint but look to God's resources and be encouraged that all you need is in Him and faith will release the answer to your prayer.

God cannot fail you; it is impossible. You often block His provision by your lack of faith and unbelief in His love. Keep believing.

Do not fear sleepless nights

Do not fear the terror of the night. When you lie down your sleep shall be sweet. Psalm 91:5

Do not fear sleepless nights. If you cannot sleep do not allow stress, panic or night tremors to prevail. Use your sleepless time productively.

1. Declare who you are in God.
2. Declare the protective blood of Jesus.
3. Declare nothing will happen to you without God's permission and that He is in control.

Sing, pray or use your prayer language and simply ignore the fears, then turn over and go to sleep!

DO NOT FEAR STEPPING OUT AND DOING
SOMETHING NEW

You say, 'I can't go out there, there is a lion in the street.'
Proverbs 22:13

Your fears can hold you back from your destiny.
Are there real lions in the street? When you want to step out and start something new you must push through the fears that present themselves. The fears may appear very real but in reality they are merely excuses for laziness and procrastination.

You can do all things through Christ who strengthens you. Push past the fear and resistance that will initially contend with you. When you take the risk and step out even in the face of fear, you will find that the fears are no longer as powerful as they appeared.
Greater is He that is in you than any fear that is in the world.

DO NOT FEAR FLOODS, LANDSLIDES OR EARTHQUAKES

Do not fear when you go through the rivers they will not overflow you'. Isaiah 43:1-3
Though mountains fall into the sea, be still and know that I am God. Psalm 46:2
Though a thousand fall at your side it shall not come near you. Psalm 91:7

When you watch the news and see the world being affected by natural disasters, do not fear. Speak the word of God over the circumstances, your life, your family and church. Come under the power of God's word and know His protection over your life.

In the day of great distress He will deliver you.

DO NOT FEAR YOUR OWN WEAKNESS

His grace is sufficient for you; for His power is made perfect in your weakness. 2 Corinthians 12:9
You can do all things through Christ who gives you the strength Philippians 4:13

Do not fear that you are not strong enough for the tasks before you. Are you afraid that your weaknesses may let you down? Then cast your weaknesses onto the Lord. Speak the word over yourself and be empowered. Joel 3:10 encourages the weak to declare, 'I am strong in the strength of the Lord my God'. Look to the Lord and His strength.

Refocus and keep your eyes on Christ and His unfailing strength and love for you.

His love for you is greater than your weaknesses.

DO NOT FEAR USING YOUR TALENTS

I was afraid and went out and hid your talent in the ground. Matthew 25:25

Do you have a gift? The hired man hid his talent in the ground out of fear. He used fear as an excuse for not multiplying his gift. We must use our gift or lose it. God turned the whole excuse around and instead of excusing the man of his fears, God accused him of laziness.

Use what you have been given and do not be afraid to step out. Write that book, do some public speaking, adopt a child, be active in mission.

Playing safe can be an excuse for laziness and if we don't use our gifts we will lose them.

Do not fear war

He makes wars cease to the ends of the earth.
Psalm 46:9
Hebrews 13:5 The Lord is my helper; I will not be
afraid.
What can man do to me? Hebrews 13:5

Do not be afraid of the news of wars or terrorist attacks. God is greater than many armies.

Matthew 24:6 says you will hear of wars and rumours of wars but be not afraid.

Remember God is still in control and greater than any nation's strength.

Do not fear being left behind

Do not let your hearts be troubled. Trust in God, trust also in Me.
In My Father's house are many rooms, if it were not so, I would have told you.
I am going to prepare a place for you. And if I go and prepare a place for you, I will comeback and take you to be with Me that you also may be where I am, John 14:1-3

Jesus said, 'I am the way, the truth and the life. No one comes to the Father except through me.' When you invite Jesus into your heart He comes in and brings eternity with Him. When He comes into your life a new relationship is formed and He knows those who are His. When He comes back He will know you and take you to be with Him.

Do not fear God's guidance

He will be our guide even unto death. Psalm 48:14

There are three keys that are crucial to knowing and following the will of God.

1 The voice of God

You shall hear a voice behind you saying, 'This is the way walk in it'. Isaiah 30:21

Be willing to listen and be still to hear the quiet voice of the Holy Spirit.

2 Keep in the word of God

His word will shed light on your way and confirm what the Spirit is saying to your Spirit.

3 Be led by the peace of God

Let your decisions be made in peace. If you lose your peace take a step back and check your decision again.

DO NOT FEAR BEING PUT TO SHAME

Those who look to Him are radiant, their faces are never covered with shame. Psalm 34:5

When you dwell on your past or present sin, you will experience shame. Jesus died on the cross to take away all your sin and shame, and does not want you to fear it when you are in Christ. Isaiah 54:4 says you shall not be put to shame and you shall forget the shame of your youth.

Psalm 23:6 says, 'goodness and mercy shall follow me all the days of my life'.

Do not fear, God has you covered.

Do not fear what is coming on the world

Men will faint from the terror that is coming on the world. Luke 21:26

Fear is a destructive and disempowering force. You cannot walk in fear and faith at the same time.

You need to be constantly reminding yourself of God's promise that He will never leave you or forsake you.

When the fears press in, trust Him; you are safe in the palms of His hands forever.

Do not fear losing your parents

I will be a Father to you. Though my father and mother forsake me, the Lord will receive me.
Psalm 27:10

Circumstances may cause you to lose your parents, physically, spiritually or emotionally. At these times it is important to remember that God is able to be both father and mother to you if you find yourself alone. God wants you to know Him as your Father and he wants to be the one to provide for you and protect you.

God can be both a mother and father to you if you cast yourself on Him who cares for you.
Ask God for the revelation of His Father heart for you today.

DO NOT FEAR PHYSICAL PAIN

By His stripes you are healed. Isaiah 53:5

Do you live with pain? Have you had a traumatic experience of physical pain? Do not fear it. Give God your fears and your pain.

Pray for the healing touch of Jesus for He said He has taken your sickness and pain on the cross. Renounce every symptom of pain the enemy is manifesting in your body and tell them to 'Go' in Jesus' Name.

DO NOT FEAR THE MEMORY OF PAIN

'Surely he took up our pain and carried our sorrows'.
Isaiah 53:4

Have you suffered a trauma or accident that was extremely painful and the memories created by fear? Maybe the memories or nightmares even produce the same pain as the first encounter. Jesus will deliver you from the pain, the memories and the nightmares.

Say this prayer: 'Thank you Lord Jesus for your healing from the painful memories I am having.
In Jesus Name I command all spirits and memories of pain, trauma and shock to leave my body, Amen'

Do not fear flooding

When you go through the floods of difficulty you shall not drown for I am with you. Isaiah 43:3

Do not fear floods or tsunamis for God is in control of the raging of the waves and rules over them. Speak God's protection over yourself daily and trust in His love for you. Perfect love casts out fear.

Speak Psalm 91 over yourself and others and stay in peace.

DO NOT FEAR FAILING GOD

To Him who is able to keep your from falling and to present you before His glorious presence without fault and with great joy. Jude 1:24

God promised to keep you strong to the end so that you will be blameless on the day of our Lord Jesus Christ. Your life and walk is in God's hands. Commit yourself and your plans afresh to God and trust Him to keep you when you cannot keep yourself.

He delights to see you come through strong to the end. Have faith in God He is able!

DO NOT FEAR LOSING FAITH IN GOD

Looking unto Jesus the author and finisher of your faith. Hebrews 12:2

Do not be afraid that your faith will fail you. He who called you is faithful. It was God who initiated faith in you. He is faithful to keep you even in trying times.

What God began in you He is able to finish and complete. Trust and commit your faith to the Holy Spirit and ask Him for faith to believe. Renounce all doubts and know that God is a faithful God.

DO NOT FEAR LOSING FRIENDS

Paul said, "No man stood with me but everyone deserted me'.
King David found strength in the Lord His God when all men turned against him. 2 Timothy 4:16

When friends leave you or fail you trust in Him who will never leave, abandon, fail or forsake you. God will be faithful when others fail you and He will stand with you and strengthen you until the trial passes.

God says "Fear not for I am with you, do not be discouraged for I am your God and will hold your right hand. Isaiah 41:10

Do not fear the power of sin

"When you were dead in your sins, God made you alive with Christ". Colossians 2:14

Do not fear sin having power over you. God made you alive with Christ. He forgave all your sins having cancelled the written code that was against you; He took it away, nailing it to the cross.

Jesus took our place of judgment for sin. He paid the price for our sins, He broke sin's power over our lives and He made a way out for us. Sin no longer has dominion over you, sin's power over you has been broken.

Who will free me from this body of death? Thanks be to God – through Jesus Christ our Lord!

DO NOT FEAR TORTURE OR PERSECUTION

Do not be afraid of those who kill the body but cannot kill the soul. Fear God only. Matthew 10:28

God will either deliver you from your enemies or give you the strength and endurance to go through a time of testing. Not everyone is called to go through physical persecution. God certainly does not want you to live in fear of what may or may not happen.

Submit your concerns to God and receive His peace. He will not fail you or forsake you. He will prepare you for what you would have to endure for Him.

Be at Peace!

DO NOT FEAR THE DARK

———◆———

Jesus said, ' I am the Light of the World; whoever follows me will never walk in darkness but will have the Light of Life. John 8:12

Do not gloat over me, my enemy! Though I sit in darkness the Lord will be my light. If I say surely the darkness will hide me and the light become night around me even the darkness will not be dark to You. The night will shine like the day, for darkness is as light to you. Psalm 139:11–12

There is no darkness too great to hide you from God. Do not fear it but pray and sing and Christ will lift the darkness and be your light. When you trust in the protection of His love all fear will go.

'Do not be afraid of any man.' Deuteronomy 1:17

DO NOT FEAR YOUR ENEMIES

Do not be afraid I am your shield and your very great reward. Genesis 15:1

Do not fear your enemies or the backlash of your enemies. God Himself is your shield and will protect you.

God will reward your faith in Him; keep moving forward holding onto His promises. Keep standing in God and outlast your enemies; God will make a way.

When a man's ways please the Lord He makes even His enemies to be at peace with him.
Proverbs 16:17

Do not fear carrying out God's plans

I know the plans I have for you, declares the Lord.
Plans to prosper you and not to harm you, plans to
give you a future and a hope. Jeremiah 29:11

Step out into God's plans even if they seem contrary
to the plans of man. God's plans for you are bigger
than man's plans for you; to obey God is more
important than to fear man. Jesus says that anyone
who loves his father or mother more than Him is not
worthy of Him.

God's plans for you may not make sense to everyone
or to you, but they will always be to bless and
prosper you, Trust Him for the outworking of His
plans for you even when things look perplexing.

DO NOT FEAR INADEQUACY

I can do all things through Christ who gives me strength. Philippians 4:13

Do not let the fear of inadequacy stop you achieving all God has for you. Lack of qualifications, personal abilities or personality cannot stop the plan and purpose God has for you. Continue to move forward in your calling and God will help you achieve your dreams.

Maybe you cannot see how you can achieve all that is in your heart. Delight yourself in the Lord and He will give you the desires of your heart.

Immerse yourself in Him and He will do what you cannot. Everything will flow out of Him. Now unto Him who is able to do immeasurably more than all we could ask for or imagine.

DO NOT FEAR BEING EXILED OR REJECTED

"Do not be afraid God has heard the boy crying."
Genesis 21:17

Hagar was in the desert watching her son starve to death and God said, 'Fear Not' and provided her with water so the boy could live. Her son symbolised all that she had; her vision, her dream, her future and her inheritance. She was afraid of watching all that die.

The dream you are carrying will not die but live to the glory of God. Man's rejection brings God's promotion.

God will provide all you need even in a dry and barren place. He will keep His word to you and you will live and bring glory to God.

DO NOT FEAR WHAT YOU ARE GOING TO SAY

Jesus said, 'Do not worry what to say, God will give you the right words at the right time'. Matthew 10:19
God said, 'Open your mouth wide and I will fill it'.
Psalms 81:10

He will provide you with wisdom and the right thing to say at the time you need it. He will go before you and change people and situations as you commit everything to Him.

Commit your way to the Lord, trust in Him and He will act on your behalf. He is faithful and amazing at diffusing difficult situations.

Do not fear spiritual darkness

Let him who walks in the dark, who has no light, trust in the name of the Lord Isaiah 50:10

If your way seems dark and you cannot see the way ahead simply wait in faith until God's light shines in the darkness. Do not get impatient and try to light your own fires, this will hinder the guidance of God.

He is honoured when we trust Him when we cannot see the way forward. He has promised that we will not stumble in the dark but will have the light of life.

DO NOT FEAR GETTING OUT OF THE BOAT

Then Peter got down out of the boat, walked on the water and came towards Jesus. Matthew 14:29

Is Jesus calling you out of your comfort zone? Do not be afraid to step out and take a risk. Do not settle when God has called you to move out.

Do not be afraid to leave the familiar and step into something new. Abraham stepped out not knowing where he was going and God was faithful.

There will never be a convenient time to step out in God. You will have to step out on the waves and God will be there.

Do not fear loneliness

God said, 'I will never fail you or forsake you'.

You will never be lonely as you keep close to God. There is a purpose and a plan for you. You will never be lonely while there are so many people to love.

Give and it shall be given to you. Invite to dinner those who cannot repay you and you shall be blessed in ways you cannot imagine.

Look out for God in the stranger, the lost and the poor.

DO NOT FEAR THE TRAUMA OF YOUR PAST

The Lord who delivered me from the paw of the lion and the paw of the bear will deliver me from the hand of this Philistine. 1 Samuel 17:37

Do not fear. God said to Noah that He would never flood the earth again. Never again would Moses see the enemies that had come against him, once he crossed the Red Sea.

That thing in your past that was sent to destroy you will ultimately be used to propel you into your destiny and you will make God famous!

Do not fear getting hurt again

Lord, you will keep us safe and protect us.
Psalm 13:7-8

Because you have been hurt in the past does not mean God will not protect you in the future.

God has promised He will not fail you or forsake you. This time you will not be going in your own strength or pride. Instead your weakness will activate God's power. For His power shows up best in weak people.

The weaker you are, the more He will carry you and display His strength through you.

DO NOT FEAR LIARS

You will condemn every tongue that accuses you. Isaiah 54:17

God said the mouths of liars would be stopped. Jesus is more powerful than any lie that has been unleashed against you. He is the way, the truth and the life and He will set you free from the lie.

No weapon fashioned against you shall prosper. God will expose the lies if you stay submitted to Him. Do not fight in the flesh but leave the lie in God's hand and He will vindicate you.

DO NOT FEAR THOSE IN AUTHORITY OVER YOU

First of all, that requests, prayers, intercession and thanksgiving be made for everyone. For Kings and all those in authority so that we may live peaceful and quiet lives in all godliness and holiness. 1 Timothy 2:1

Do not fear those whom God has placed over you. People in authority are put there by God and He lifts up and brings down. Proverbs 21:1 says the King's heart is in the hand of the Lord, Like the rivers of water; He turns it wherever He wishes. Do not slander or rebel against those over you.

Honour those over you and fear only God and He will deliver you from the hands of those who oppress you.

DO NOT FEAR LOSING YOUR CHILDREN

I will contend with those who contend with you and your children I will save. Isaiah 49:24

Do you fear that your children are at risk in any way? Bring your fears to the Lord for there is one that is mightier who will fight for you and your children. Keep bringing your children and their needs before the throne of God.

Do not fear losing your children to custody, drugs, lifestyle or another person, for God is mighty to save.

Do not fear sharing the gospel

Go into all the world and preach the good news to all creation. Mark 16:15

The Holy Spirit does not want you to be afraid of people. He wants you to be wise and strong in Him and to love people. Jesus said, 'If anyone publicly acknowledges Me as their friend, I will openly acknowledge them as My friend before My Father in heaven.'

Ask God to fill you with the power of the Holy Spirit as He filled the disciples. Then you can be a witness of the gospel of Jesus Christ.

Ask for divine opportunities today to share your faith and overcome your fears.

DO NOT FEAR GLOBAL WARMING

'The sun shall not smite you by day or the moon by night.' Psalm 121:6

Do you fear the ozone-layer getting worse, the sun getting hotter, lack of water or other weather news? The sun, moon, stars and weather are all under God's authority and He gave us all authority over the earth to subdue it.

When the disciples were afraid of the storm Jesus spoke to the storm and commanded it to be still. He then rebuked the disciples for their little faith for He expected them to take authority over the elements themselves.

Ask God for the faith to walk in the authority you have been given and not to be afraid of the changing weather conditions.

DO NOT FEAR HEART ATTACKS

My flesh and my heart may fail me but God is the strength of my heart and my portion forever.
Psalm 73:26

The Lord gives strength to His people, the Lord blesses His people with peace. Psalm 29:11

By His wounds we are healed. Isaiah 53:5

Confess these scriptures over yourself every day and believe God for a strong healthy heart both physically, emotionally and spiritually.

The word of God gives life and He is the strength of your heart.

Do not fear the call of leadership

I will make you strong, Go I am sending you!
Judges 6:12

Do you fear being asked to step up into a leadership role? Do you want to back out of a leadership role you have been put in? God says, 'Lead on with strength and courage. Do not give up or give in. I am with you, My power shows up best in your weakness.'

I have called you as a leader and I have equipped you to overcome any fear in your life. Whether it is fear of rejection, failure of a task, shame, criticism, being out of control or making mistakes.

You have not been given a spirit of intimidation as a leader but a spirit of love, power and a sound mind. Stay faithful to the leadership call and I will bless and strengthen you.

DO NOT FEAR MOVING TO A NEW AREA

See, I am sending my angel ahead of you to guard you along the way and to bring you to the place I have prepared. Exodus 23:20

Do not give in to the fear of a new house, new neighbours or a new environment. God has already gone ahead of you and is working in every detail of your life before you even get there. You will be amazed at the big and little surprises that God has stored up for you in your new home.

He has gone ahead to prepare jobs, friends, schools, transport, church and whatever else you may need. Give Him every burden and every fear and 'keep moving' forward in peace to your new home.

DO NOT FEAR ILLNESS OR DISEASE

Jesus cursed the fig tree and it withered from the roots.
Mark 11:20

Every condition has a root and Jesus dealt with roots at the cross.

One day Jesus cursed a fig tree at its root and the fig tree immediately died from the roots. Speak to your condition and command it to go and be plucked up by the roots in Jesus' name. Curse the root of sickness attacking you. Even faith the size of a grain of mustard seed will move it.

Do not fear not being accepted by God

If you do what is right ; will you not be accepted.
Genesis 4: 6

Cain feared he would not be accepted by God, but God reached down and attempted to restore their fellowship. Cain was jealous of his brother Abel because he feared God loved Abel more than him. But it was not true. God does not have favourites; He is no respecter of men.

Nothing can separate us from the love of God which is in Christ Jesus our Lord. Jesus told Peter he was not to worry about what God was doing with somebody else, but to follow Him.

Keep focused on Jesus; He will never reject you.

Do not fear being cast away from God

If we confess our sins, He is faithful and just and will forgive us our sins and cleanse us from all unrighteousness. 1 John 1:9

If you believe you have grieved God there is always a way back. Jesus Himself is interceding for you. Do not fear you have committed the unpardonable sin. Go to Jesus with a repentant heart; He promised He would never reject those who come to Him.

If you have sinned you can confess your sin. He promised to forgive your sin and cleanse you from all unrighteousness. There is always a way back to God.

Do not fear other people's success or promotion

From that time on Saul kept a jealous eye on David
1 Samuel 18:9

When Saul saw how successful David was he was afraid of him. You can allow fear to enter your life when you are jealous of someone else's success.

Other people's promotion and success can be threatening; perfect love towards others will cast out your fear.

Saul never did overcome the jealousy he had towards David and it cost him everything. Ask God to deliver you from the spirit of jealousy and focus on the plan God has for your life.

Do not fear creatures big or small

God blessed them and said to them, 'Rule over the fish of the sea and the birds of the air and over every living creature that moves on the ground.' Genesis 1:28

You have been given authority and dominion over every creature. You are called to subdue and rule over every creature from insects to lions. Every creature is under your dominion and rule in Christ.

David killed a bear and a lion and Paul shook off a deadly snake that had bitten him. Jesus said He has given you power to tread on scorpions and serpents and nothing shall hurt you.

When you keep in God's love His protection is with you, even over insects and animals.

DO NOT FEAR CURSES

A curse causeless falls. Proverbs 26:2
All these blessings will come upon you if you obey
the Lord Your God. Deuteronomy 28:2

Jesus was made a curse for you. You do not have
to fear curses when you walk in obedience to God
because obedience is a powerful force in breaking
curses over your life.

If you do believe that a curse is over you seek out
a minister who can pray with you.

'Do not be afraid and do not be
discouraged for the Lord your God
will be with you wherever you go.'
Joshua 1:9

DO NOT FEAR GOD'S PROMISES TO YOU WILL DIE

Hagar was promised that her son would become a great nation. Genesis 21:18

Hagar was faced with watching her son die in a sun scorched wilderness. As Hagar turned away from her son God spoke to her. He reaffirmed His promise to Hagar that her son would become a great nation.

It was not because of Hagar's cry that the promise of God was stirred, it was the cry of the boy, Ishmael. God hears His promises cry out from you and He will not let them die, but will bring them to fulfillment.

DO NOT FEAR PUTTING YOUR
DREAM ON THE ALTAR

Abraham was asked to take his son and lay him on the altar. Genesis 22:2

Abraham obeyed instantly and put Isaac on the altar even though God had promised to bless Abraham through his son. Abraham would not have understood this command but he trusted God to keep His promise. He even expected God to raise Isaac from the dead.

God never intended to kill the promise He made to Abraham. He needed to know that He was loved and worshipped by Abraham for who He was, not just for His promises.

Is the promise of God more important to you than God Himself? If you never got your promise, would you still worship Him? God wants your dream to live and not die; do not fear.

DO NOT FEAR TEMPTATION BECOMING TOO STRONG FOR YOU

God is faithful; He will not let you be tempted beyond what you can bear. 1 Corinthians 10:13

Temptation to do wrong can appear too strong for us at times, but the word says there is always a way of escape.

If you are faced with overwhelming temptation today ask God to show you the escape route and run! Do not try and resist temptation on your own. Commit the situation to God and if you have someone over you that you can trust, ask for prayer.

God will make a way of escape for you before the temptation leads you to a dead end.

Do not fear someone stealing your dream

When Jesus knew it was time to leave this world He passed His mission onto His disciples. He told them they would do even greater works than He had done. Is your ministry or dream for Jesus or for your own glory? The only way to know if your ministry or dream is owned by God, is by how willing you are to pass on the baton to someone else, rather than let it die.

There were two women in the days of King Solomon who fought over the same baby. The baby only belonged to one of the mothers. King Solomon found out who the true mother was by commanding it's death. The true mother would rather hand the baby over to someone else than let the baby die. Your dream must be bigger than you and you must be able to trust God to keep your dream alive.

Do not fear Failure

For though the righteous fall seven times, they rise again. Proverbs 24:16

Failure is an event and not a person. To fail at an attempt does not make you a failure.

There are no failures with God, only more opportunities. The only way is up!

Get up one more time. You may be knocked down but not out! Who knows your next attempt could be your finest hour?

Never, never, never give up!

Do not fear going back

If God tells you to go back to a place you have
previously left, do not fear.

God told Moses to go back to Egypt but because of
his past record Moses was afraid to go.   God
encouraged Moses by saying those who had meant
him harm were no longer a threat.

God moves people in and out of your life. If He has
called you back to a past place, do not fear meeting
those you left behind.

God will make it a new day for you.

Do not fear acting on what you believe

Faith without works is dead. James 2:17

Do not be afraid to step out and act on what you believe you should be doing. It may be a ministry, career or course. It may be to share your faith or invite someone to church. Maybe you believe you have a book, a song or a testimony inside you. Do something about it and act today.

Good intentions will accomplish nothing. It is what you do that counts.

DO NOT FEAR FALSE ACCUSATIONS

When Jesus was accused by the chief priests and the elders, He gave no answer. Matthew 27:12

Intimidation can come through false accusations. These accusations are sent to stop, block or delay the work God has called you to do. Keep doing what you are called to do and do not allow the work of God to come to a standstill.

Do not try and vindicate yourself, place yourself in the hands of Almighty God and keep a right heart before Him and He will vindicate you! Be patient and see the salvation of the Lord and the exposure of the false accusations.

Do not fear speaking for God because of age

Do not say, 'I am young' but say whatever I command you. Jeremiah 1:7
Do not let anyone look down on you because you are young; be an example in speech. 1 Timothy 1:2
Moses said, 'I have never been eloquent and am slow of speech.' The Lord said to Moses, 'Go, I will help you speak and tell you what to say.' Exodus 4:10

Do not let age or ability hold you back from obeying God and speaking for Him. You may be called to speak in Church, at work, or college. Do not let fear overcome you. Give your concerns to God, prepare well and trust Him. When you open your mouth God will fill it and give you the confidence you need.

God promises to be strong in your weakness.

Do not fear the fiery trial

Though now for a little while you may have to suffer grief in all kinds of trials. These have come so that your faith of greater worth than gold, may be proved genuine. And may result in praise, glory and honour when Jesus Christ is revealed. 1 Peter 1:6-7

To have the fire of God you need to go through the fire. The trials you are going through are serving a Kingdom purpose. However painful the trial, keep doing what is right and keep faith in God; he will bring you through as pure gold.

The fire of God will not destroy you but it will refine and equip you for His service. Remember to keep praising Him in the midst of the fiery trial and you will come out with not even the smell of fire on you! He has not left you, He is in the fire with you!

DO NOT FEAR LACK OF STRENGTH

He gives strength to the weary and increases the power
of the weak Isaiah 40:29
When I am weak then I am strong. 2 Corinthians 12:10

King David was always honest with God when he felt his strength had failed him, and God was always quick to remind David that He was his strength. God promised that you would have adequate strength for each day.

Speak to yourself every day and say, 'I am strong in the strength of the Lord God,' and 'I can do all things through Christ who gives me the strength.' Remind yourself constantly that your strength must come from the Lord's mighty power within you.

You do not have to be physically strong to be strong in the Lord. But is is good to keep your body in good condition, so you can carry out God's work to the best of your ability.

DO NOT FEAR GOING BACK TO WORK

He who works his land will have abundant food.
Proverbs 28:19

If you have been out of work for a season and know you must go back, then take courage and take the first step. Look for a vacancy, make some calls, ask your minister to pray with you. Do whatever it takes to overcome the procrastination, fear or laziness that may have set in during your time off work.

Do not fear rejection as you apply for new jobs; every step forward will bring fresh courage. The worst thing you can do is to stay where you are and do nothing!

Do not fear Jesus' return

We who are still alive and are left will be caught up together with them in the clouds to meet the Lord in the air. Therefore encourage each other with these words.
1 Thessalonians 4:18

Do not live in fear of when Jesus may return, instead be encouraged that you are His and it will be a joyful reunion. We are told in God's word to encourage each other with these words and not to put fear into each other. You should not fear the end of the world, but look forward to Jesus' return in all His glory and majesty.

You will see the Son of Man coming on the clouds of the sky with power and great glory. You must be ready because the Son of Man will come at an hour when you do not expect Him.

Do not fear cancer

I will say of the Lord He is my refuge. Surely He will save you from the deadly pestilence. You will not fear the terror of night nor the arrow that flies by day, nor the pestilence that stalks in the darkness nor the plague that destroys at midday. Psalm 91:3

When you are faced with a negative doctor's diagnosis, do not let the words take root in your heart. Immediately ask God for a scripture or promise and declare 'I shall not die but live to the glory of God'.

Ask your ministers to anoint you will oil according to James 5 and believe God for your miracle. Speak the work of God over your life constantly and do not allow the negative, fearful thoughts of the enemy to reign in your mind. Shut them out with the word.

God says in Psalm 91:14 'Because he loves Me, I will rescue him, I will be with him in trouble and I will deliver him and honour him. With long life will I satisfy him and show him my salvation.

'Do not be afraid or discouraged.
Go out to face them tomorrow and
the Lord will be with you.'
2 Chronicles 20 :17

Do not fear discouragement

Then the people around them set out to discourage the people
of Judah and make them afraid to go on building.
Ezra 4: 4

Do not fear the discouragement that comes your way
when you are seeking to obey God. God will give you the
encouragement you need or send others into your life to
stand with you.

Do not give into the enemy's wishes and back down or
retreat from doing the thing you are called to do. Any
opposition you are facing will only be seasonal. Outlast
your discouragement and remind yourself that God will
never, never fail you or forsake you.

Discouragement is the opposite of courage so take
strength in the Lord and keep going: do not retreat!

DO NOT FEAR DEPRESSION

Why are you so depressed my soul? Why so disturbed within? Put your hope in God for you will yet praise Him. Psalm 42:5

King David knew what is felt like to be depressed and the first thing he did was to speak to himself and declare the word over himself. When depressing thoughts come it is usually because you are looking inward and not outwards. Do not allow self pity to feed the depression.

Remind yourself that whatever is causing you to be depressed will give you an opportunity for praise; if you continue to trust in God. If the depression persists find a friend, minister or a professional to come alongside and give some support. Remember, the joy of the Lord is your strength.

DO NOT FEAR TRANSITION

When evening came the boat was in the middle of the lake and the disciples were straining at the oars, because the wind was against them. Jesus came to them and said, 'Take courage! It is I. Don't be afraid' Mark 6:47

The disciples were in the middle of the lake. They had left the security and comfort of the shore but the storm was so great they did not think they would make it to their destination.

Transition can feel like this for you. When God calls you out of your comfort zone He does not automatically plant you in your new sphere of influence. It can seem as though you have been left to survive on your own. It is easy to wonder where God is and what is going on.

But God has not left you to struggle alone. He will come to you and suddenly the storm will die down. Suddenly you will reach your destination. To trust God in transition prepares you for the promotion He has for you ahead. He will not fail you.

DO NOT FEAR GETHSEMANE

Jesus went to a place called Gethsemane and said, 'My soul is overwhelmed with sorrow to the point of death.' Matthew 26:36-39

Gethsemane is the place of intense pressure and sorrow. A place where even if your friends are around they cannot help you. It is a lonely, heartbreaking place. It is a place of decision; your will or God's!

Jesus came to a place of total surrender to the cross by saying to God, 'not my will but Yours be done.' Beware of making decisions under pressure that would cause you to preempt God's will in your life. When you are under intense pressure, submit yourself to God and He will strengthen you.

Do not fear hunger

Jesus answered, 'Man does not live on bread alone, but on every word that comes from the mouth of God.'
Matthew 4:4

Jesus had been fasting for forty days and nights and would have been hungry. He could have commanded the stones to turn to bread, but he refused. Hunger comes in many forms: physical, emotional, spiritual, financial, relational, the list goes on. Jesus knew there was more to life than simply satisfying a temporal need.

God will meet every legitimate need in your life, do not fear. Do not give into the temptation to turn your stones into bread. Wait on God, for He supplies all your need according to His riches in glory. Do not shortcut an answer to your need by trying to fill your own hunger.

DO NOT FEAR YOUR SONS OR DAUGHTERS
MOVING AWAY

Do not fear I will bring your sons and daughters back from afar. Isaiah 43:6

Do not fear the news that your son or daughter may be moving far away. Commit them into God's hands and plan for their lives; then trust God that He will bring them back. Do not let fear reign over the situation but have faith that God is bigger than any plan man can make.

As we make the Lord our delight, He gives us the desires of our heart and if that is to be reunited with our children, He knows.

Do not fear those who plan evil against you

Do not fret because of evil men... I have seen a wicked and ruthless man flourishing like a green tree, but he soon passed away and was no more; though I looked for him, he could not be found. Psalm 37:1, 35-36

Do not fear those in your life who are controlling you or trying to cause you trouble. No matter how long they have had power in your life it will not be forever.

God has His day of deliverance and the wicked that seem so powerful, one day you will see no more. The Lord helps and delivers you from the wicked because you take refuge in Him.

DO NOT FEAR DELAYS TO PRAYER

*Do not fear, Daniel, since the first day you prayed;
your words were heard.
But the Prince of Persia resisted me twenty-one days.
Daniel 10:12*

Do not start to fear when your prayers do not seem to be answered. It is not always God holding back your blessing or not hearing your prayers. There is often a resistance from the enemy trying to hold back your blessing.

Daniel began fasting and this gave power to his prayers. Maybe you can fast something to show God that you are fervent about your prayer requests. Delays are not denials. God wants to bless you and answer your prayers.

Do not fear stepping out in later years

God said to Jacob, 'Do not be afraid to go down to Egypt, I will make you into a great nation there. I will go down to Egypt with you.' Genesis 46:4

God told Jacob in his latter years to leave his house and everything that was familiar and go to a faraway land. Moving out in faith when you are older is quite different to moving out in faith when you are younger. But God promised Jacob He would go with him.

God's promise to you of His leading and faithfulness never changes with age. It is with you every time you step out in obedience to His revealed will.

Do not fear being hemmed in

Then he sent a strong force and they went by night and surrounded the city. When the servant of the man of God got up and went out the next morning a force had surrounded the city. "Oh, my Lord, what shall we do? the servant asked. "Don't be afraid", the prophet answered. "Those who are with us are more than those who are with them". Then the Lord opened the servants eyes and he looked and saw the hills full of horses and chariots of fire all around Elisha. 2 Kings 6 : 14

Jesus prays to God in John 17:15 and asks God to keep His disciples safe from Satan's power.

When Jehoshaphat was surrounded on all sides by enemy forces he was told not to fear. God told Jehoshaphat not to fear but to stand still and see God deliver him. When you feel afraid; pray. Trust God that He will deliver you from those who are too strong for you.

Made in the USA
Charleston, SC
11 February 2013